# Around & About
# Roborough Down

## Chips Barber

## OBELISK PUBLICATIONS

## Also by the Author

Diary of a Dartmoor Walker
Diary of a Devonshire Walker
Ten Family Walks on Dartmoor
Ten Family Walks in East Devon
Six Short Pub Walks on Dartmoor
The Great Little Dartmoor Book
The Great Little Chagford Book
Beautiful Dartmoor
Dark and Dastardly Dartmoor
Weird and Wonderful Dartmoor
Cranmere Pool – The First Dartmoor Letterbox
The Teign Valley of Yesteryear, Parts I and II
Princetown of Yesteryear, Parts I and II
Widecombe – A Visitor's Guide
Railways on and around Dartmoor
Around & About Tavistock
Along The Tavy

## Other Dartmoor Titles

The Great Walks of Dartmoor, *Terry Bound*
The A to Z of Dartmoor Tors, *Terry Bound*
Walks in the Chagford Countryside, *Terry Bound*
Walks in the Shadow of Dartmoor, *Denis McCallum*
Walks in Tamar and Tavy Country, *Denis McCallum*
The Templer Way, *Derek Beavis*
The Dartmoor Mountain Bike Guide, *Peter Barnes*
Circular Walks on Eastern Dartmoor, *Liz Jones*
Under Sail Through South Devon and Dartmoor, *Raymond B. Cattell*

*We have over 150 Devon titles. For a full list of current books, please contact us at Obelisk Publications, 2 Church Hill, Pinhoe, Exeter, Devon, EX4 9ER or telephone (01392) 468556.*

## Acknowledgements

Thanks to Sue and Richard Callow for pictures on pages 5, 6, 7 (bottom), 8 (top left) and 11; Jill Fitzsimmons for pages 29 (top), 31 and 32; *Western Morning News* for 16 (top) and 24 (top). All other pictures by or belonging to Chips Barber.

*First published in 1998 by*
*Obelisk Publications, 2 Church Hill, Pinhoe, Exeter, Devon*
*Designed by Chips and Sally Barber*
*Typeset by Sally Barber*
*Printed in Great Britain by*
*The Devonshire Press Ltd, Torquay, Devon*

# Around & About

# Roborough Down

As the title would suggest, this book features Roborough Down and the rivers, rocks, mines, railways, quarries, pubs, hamlets, houses and villages in its vicinity. This includes brief glimpses of Buckland Monachorum, Buckland Abbey, Clearbrook, Yelverton, Horrabridge, Dousland, Roborough, Bickleigh, Milton Combe, Meavy, Walkhampton and Shaugh Prior, not forgetting the countryside in between!

We will start at one of the most visited and distinct landmarks of Roborough Down, a gently undulating plateau with a general top elevation of about 600 feet above sea level. Roborough Rock is an outcrop of magnesium limestone, in places almost worn smooth by visitors, who love to scramble over it. Although today it has the simplest and most obvious name of all, it has had other names in the past, including Hurlestone Rock, Ullestor, Yelverton Rock, Udal Tor and Yudel Tor. It's small wonder that folk have now settled for 'The Rock'. To avoid confusion with the pub of the same name in nearby Yelverton, this outcrop is known as the 'Dry Rock' whilst the pub is the 'Wet Rock', such is the genius of simplicity. Terry Bound, in his excellent book *The A to Z of Dartmoor Tors,* included the following as part of the entry for this non-conforming tor: *"One long mass of rock on level ground, this tor is on the edge of the National Park. It is not difficult to find … park next to it! It is a kilometre from Yelverton roundabout on the A386 Plymouth Road. On the OS map, six inches to one mile, a house situated 140 metres northwest of the rock is named Udal Torre, but the rock itself is called Roborough."*

Perhaps the most famous of all Dartmoor writers, William Crossing (1847–1928), had this to say of it: *"On the slope between the eighth and ninth milestones is Roborough Rock. It's shown on the eighteenth century map of Devon as Ullestor Rock, but early in the nineteenth was scarcely ever called by that name. It consists of two bosses, with a connecting portion of some length and of much less elevation, the whole forming one mass. On the northern side of the eastern boss a rude resemblance to the human face in profile may be traced when seen from the road. In my early days this was always called the Duke of Wellington's Nose."* Crossing also recalled this part of

Roborough Down where he spent his childhood holidays in a cottage. *"One of my earliest recollections is a walk from the cottage referred to past Roborough Rock to that part of the down between the entrances to Bickham and Maristowe, to which I was taken by father, to see some military manoeuvres. This was in 1854, and among the troops was a Highland regiment, which shortly after left England for the Crimea. For several years Roborough Down remained as I knew it; then a few houses were built on the Horrabridge road, and at length with the opening of the Princetown railway came the development of the present residential neighbourhood ...*

*Roborough Down, on the verge of which the residences forming Yelverton are situated, extends from the sixth milestone from Plymouth to about the tenth, the continuation of the common, which makes a northwesterly sweep to the Tavy forming Buckland Down."* This latter term seems to have lapsed from common usage.

More troops gathered on Roborough Down in the summer of 1873 for training exercises. These were first inspected by the Duke of Cambridge. However, on 21 August 1873 there was a Grand Review and March Past, which was carried out on Roborough Down before the Prince of Wales and the Duke of Edinburgh.

That summer had been a particularly wet one and the rivers in the district, the Tavy, Walkham, Plym and Meavy, were all swollen. Unfortunately two officers got into difficulties trying to cross Gratton Ford on the Meavy. Although both men made it to the far bank, one of them, Colonel Mackenzie, died before help arrived. It was later concluded that the cause of death was "owing to syncope [a temporary loss of consciousness caused by a fall in blood pressure], aggravated by immersion and exhaustion".

An early-nineteenth-century sailor had to walk from Tavistock to board his ship at Plymouth. Along the way he became tired and decided to have a sleep at Roborough Rock. Having dozed awhile he continued across the Down towards Plymouth. A few miles down the road he realised that his purse was missing but because of the time he couldn't go back to look for it. Three long years later, having travelled thousands of miles around the globe, the sailor found himself doing the reverse walk from Plymouth to Tavistock. On approaching Roborough Rock he recalled his last costly visit. As one would, he looked in the area where he had slept and was amazed to discover his purse in a fissure of the Rock! These days, with the sheer number of people clambering over it, particularly at weekends, a re-enactment of this 'lost and found' saga is most unlikely.

A type of stone embedded across Roborough Down is a fine-grained elvan material (quartz porphyry, formed about 220–260 million years ago) which was used in many buildings in the district. It can be seen in parts of churches at Tamerton Foliot, Shaugh Prior, Plympton St Mary, Plympton St Maurice and also at Whitchurch, to name but some. This stone, with a pitted appearance, was also cut and carved for troughs and mortars. With a warmer appearance than purer granite, light grey with a touch of buff and without sparkle, it was also ideal for carved work, window mullions, church arcades, dressings and so on, and was much acclaimed in medieval times. It was obviously a prized stone because it was often carried quite a distance to be used, and this in an age when journeys were slow and tedious. 'Roborough Stone', as it was known, was extracted from dykes crossing the Down in an east–west direction. However, most of the Roborough Stone quarries have been filled in, the only visible reminders being the objects and buildings which utilised this granitic 'white' elvan.

The Rock Hotel, in Yelverton, is one of the oldest buildings in this area, parts of the building dating back to the time of Drake. An unusual factor has been the current continuity of ownership, in that one family has kept it for more than a century. In the first half of the nineteenth century it was Blatchford's Rock Hotel but in 1862 William Shillabeer took over, thereby beginning a new dynasty that was to see the building develop through several generations of his family. His daughters took over in the 1880s and promptly acquired adjacent land. On it they extended the premises and were later joined in the business, in 1905, by 27-year-old Algy Langton, a nephew. His arrival signalled the start of a run of Langtons at the helm which has continued ever since, although Algy left it late before marrying a young hard-working Cornish girl of 24 when he was 41. The couple were tireless workers, Algy taking full control in the 1920s, and between them they built a successful business (tel no 22). From 1935 to 1966 it had a prestigious three-star rating.

Its peak decades, despite the recession, were the 1920s and 1930s when there was a huge influx of wealthy visitors. The Rock, 'One of the Most Comfortable Hotels in the West Country', was also busy in the Second World War years when many military personnel found themselves in the district.

The coming of the railways, in the 1880s, had helped Yelverton establish itself as an inland resort that also had a reputation for being a health-giving location. The *Ward Lock Guide* for 1927 said: *"The prevailing winds are westerly, and these, sweeping across the Atlantic, imbue the pure moorland air with ozone. For these reasons Yelverton is strongly recommended by doctors as a place of residence for sufferers from pulmonary complaints."* The Yelverton environment was also ideal for outdoor pursuits for those who were fit enough to enjoy them. The 'unwinding' process may have included motor tours, a round of golf, a game of tennis, a spot of otter or fox hunting, fishing or shooting, a dabble with the oil paints, an invigorating stroll; the list was extensive. When these had been ticked off the busy schedule there were the rounds of cocktails and sumptuous meals at the Rock and at other hotels. Much of the Rock's produce was home-grown from the vegetable garden at the side of the now extended premises. But the social and economic climate, in all sorts of ways, began to change soon after the Second World War.

The postwar era saw Yelverton develop further as a residential area. Houses mushroomed on the former gardens behind the Rock Hotel and therefore it was game, set and match for the tennis court, this being sacrificed for the creation of an access road to the 'new' houses. The vegetable garden became the site of a new health centre.

In 1966 it was decided to relinquish the hotel side of the business and the bedrooms were converted into residential flats. Having outlived his wife, Algy Langton died in 1970 at the age of 92 but the family link had been firmly established as his sons, George and Guy, were by then running the business. On Algy's death Guy retired and George took control of the entire concern. In 1981 Paul Langton, George's eldest son, joined the pub side of the business as a partner and in 1992 George passed his partnership to his own daughter, Susan. Her brother, James Langton, took on, from his mother, the Plume of Feathers at Princetown ... but that's another story!

The Devon Tors, 'High Reputation for Comfort and Satisfaction', is another Yelverton hotel to have seen changing times and was formed from three houses in a terrace. It is adjacent to the present roundabout and was advertised as '6 minutes walk from the railway station'. In 1910 these

properties were bought by Mr Charles Wilson, a strictly religious man, who converted the buildings into a temperance hotel (tel Yelverton 4). A visit to this former hotel must have surely been good for the soul, Charles Wilson saying grace before each meal. Over the years the Devon Tors attracted its share of visitors but in 1982 the hotel closed and the accommodation was turned over into flats with just the lower part of the premises remaining licensed, the 'temperance' tag having long passed into oblivion.

There were other establishments to cater for the tourist boom. The Moor House Hotel (tel Yelverton 36), 'Occupying the Finest Site in Yelverton' was demolished during the Second World War to make way for a new road to Tavistock. Just around the bend was the Yelverton Hotel, now the Leg O' Mutton. There were also several other 'private' hotels like the Fernleigh, 'Refurnished and Redecorated throughout' and the Beechfield which had a 'shady lawn', 'Motor-Car on hire', and 'Electric Light'! The district was awash with visitors and they were obviously well looked after.

Yelverton has influenced various writers, particularly early in the twentieth century. Eden Philpotts took it, and its immediate area, for the scene of *Some Everyday Folk*. F. Will Crofts made Yelverton the starting point for an exciting motor chase in his book *The Ponson Case* when motoring was the privilege of the wealthy.

L. A. G. Strong spent his early years at Yelverton, his father having moved to the moor for health reasons at the beginning of the twentieth century. The family residence was No 1 Beech Villas. No doubt he was inspired by his wanderings around the district, for his books reflect his childhood years. His *Dewer Rides* shows him to have had a lively imagination.

Yelverton got its own railway station in 1885, the initial line from Plymouth to Tavistock only having stations at Marsh Mills, Bickleigh and Horrabridge. The latter was the 'junction' for Princetown until Yelverton's station opened, two years after the passenger line began running to this Dartmoor high spot.

The late Victorian and Edwardian era was another boom time for Yelverton and its surrounding area because the railway made it easily accessible. The beautiful countryside was attractive, not just for a healthy holiday but an excellent one in which to live and impressive homes sprang up. The residential newcomers fell into various groups, all with money, but they all knew the social pecking order!

Crapstone saw its first houses built, notably 'Crapstone Terrace', in 1887, the Golden Jubilee Year of Queen Victoria. By 1930 this hamlet had mushroomed to 80 houses.

That 'milestone' in Queen Victoria's long reign was celebrated the length and breadth of the country. A bonfire was lit on 'Gib Hill', not far from Leg O' Mutton, and local children were treated to a grand tea at Pound, a large and impressive mansion nearby, which had been rebuilt about 1820. Ten years later, and Queen Victoria's Diamond Jubilee, saw even more celebrations. This time Buckland's farmers provided wagons for the very young and old to be brought to Leg O' Mutton Corner where a high tea was organised for hundreds of parishioners. There were sports, and all the winners were presented with commemorative medals. A bonfire was lit on Rook Hill; the village cross at Buckland was restored; and the Diamond Jubilee drinking fountain, by the Rock, was erected.

A further taste of the shape of things to come occurred on Monday, 6 December 1905 when the first car ever seen at Yelverton, or anywhere else in this area, arrived. It had been bought by the Plymouth firm of Spooners as a delivery vehicle. It arrived at Plymouth the previous day and a team of reporters were treated to a drive across Roborough Down. They recorded that some of the locals who saw this 'unique' spectacle were rendered speechless.

Leg O' Mutton is now separated from the main part of Yelverton but used to be, until the early 1900s, the main shopping area for the village. The bisection was caused by the building of new roads, and the development of shops close to the Green. But all is not lost, because the unusual and excellent Paperweight Centre, established in 1968, with its incredible display of more than 800 glass paperweights, attracts tourists all the year round. There are also a pub, places to eat and a fine newsagent to make a visit to Leg O' Mutton worthwhile.

In the 1960s and early 1970s, the café, opposite the former post office, was called the Cabin. The proprietor was the late, great Don Arnold, then a local television celebrity, one of two sports reporters for the former Westward TV (the other was David Vine).

In the 1960s there were a number of headstrong young 'bikers' in the district including, it is said, those who would put a record on the juke box at the Cabin and then attempt to ride the length

of Roborough Down, as far as the snack bar known as the Green Hut (now the Dartmoor Chef, and bigger) and then back to Leg O' Mutton before it had ended. Assuming the average '60s song lasted about three minutes, this meant a mighty dash along the then unfenced Down. The practice was said to have been abandoned when a biker lost his life in an ill-fated try at this daredevil stunt. A large cow had wandered off the Down and into his path and the rider, unable to avoid her, hit the poor creature full on. It is believed that the speedo was 'frozen' at 120 m.p.h.! Roborough Down was later wisely fenced off.

In Victorian times there used to be a public house on the same side of the road as the Cabin, in 'Buckland Terrace', called the Buller's Arms after a celebrated local family (there was also a Wheal Buller mine about half a mile away to the south west). It was established following the upgrading of the turnpike road through to Tavistock but its life as a pub was mostly limited to the late nineteenth century.

In 1902 the building opposite, a private dwelling, was converted into the Yelverton Hotel. It kept this name until 1972 when it became the Foxhunter, after a famous horse which had won the Gold Medal at the 1954 Olympic Games in Helsinki. On 1 April 1984 the name changed yet again to become, perhaps the most appropriate for the locality, the Leg O' Mutton.

Part of Roborough Down is a golf course and there cannot be many courses in Devon with such a wonderful open aspect. Any golfer who has a keen eye for the surrounding scenery can play a round, get some great exercise and have a pleasant moorland stroll all at the same time. It is a testing course because of the number of obstacles, sometimes turning potential 'birdies' into 'bogeys', in the form of the rough natural vegetation, banks, trees, an historic leat, a bomb crater, disused mine pits and various depressions in the terrain. This shouldn't be too surprising because Roborough loosely means 'Rough Hill'. However this does not detract, at all, from the loveliness of the course.

The club's history dates back to 1904 when a small band of locals established a short nine-hole course, designed by Charles Gibson of Westward Ho!, on four fields near the Down. This was later extended to eighteen holes. The legendary golfers Harry Vardon and J. J. Taylor played the first official round on the extended course on 13 May 1911, but its future was short-lived. During the First World War half of the course was ploughed up for crops. However, the golfing bug had bitten and as soon as hostilities had ceased a representation was made to the Lord of the Manor, Lord Roborough (Sir Henry Lopes), who allowed them to develop an eighteen-hole course on the Down. Top golf course designer Herbert Fowler, of Walton Heath, was invited to plan the new course. However he didn't have much control over the nineteenth hole, this being just a tin shack in those early formative years.

A feature of the course is the number of grazing animals, local farmers exercising the right to pasture them on this open land. To this end the club pays an annual sum of compensation to the Dartmoor Commoners for the disturbance they cause to the grazing animals. Technically this is not just sheep, cattle and ponies but also donkeys, pigs or goose herds! Roborough Down is still owned by the Lord of the Manor but since 1911 is partly administered by the Roborough Commoners Association. It monitors the use of Roborough Down, which also includes film makers, the Army, ice cream vendors, building developers and so on.

The thirteenth hole was a potentially more hazardous hole than most of the golfers might have imagined, at least just after the Second World War. What many thought was nothing more than a grassy hollow collapsed to reveal a deep mine pit, not the sort of 'hole in one' that any golfer would wish to have sunk! Yeoland Consols was a mine that worked under this part of Roborough Down in the latter part of the nineteenth century, almost 500 tons of black tin being extracted from quite an extensive system of shafts (not the golfing variety!). This was the first mine in the district to use a water turbine, the water for working it being drawn from the nearby, but now dry, Drake's Leat.

Anyone who has ever driven a vehicle over Roborough Down, even with the fences, will know that it is home to a large number of ponies who feed off the vegetation. They have good years and bad. A good one was 1936 and under the headlines of "Pony Drift at Roborough – Picturesque Scene On The Moor – Fine Collection of the Breed" an article was published giving us an insight into how these ponies were rounded up on 25 September of that year.

*"Strings of Dartmoor ponies, with streaming manes, galloped across Roborough Down when the commoners held a 'round-up' yesterday. It was the first pony drift arranged by Mr R. Hamley, secretary to Roborough Commoners, and he intends to organize another next spring.*

*Rarely have the ponies been in finer condition, for the wet season has meant plenty of grass, and the mounted Commoners on horseback who drove them to Mr G. Elford's field at Shaugh remarked they had never had so much trouble in getting them in before.*

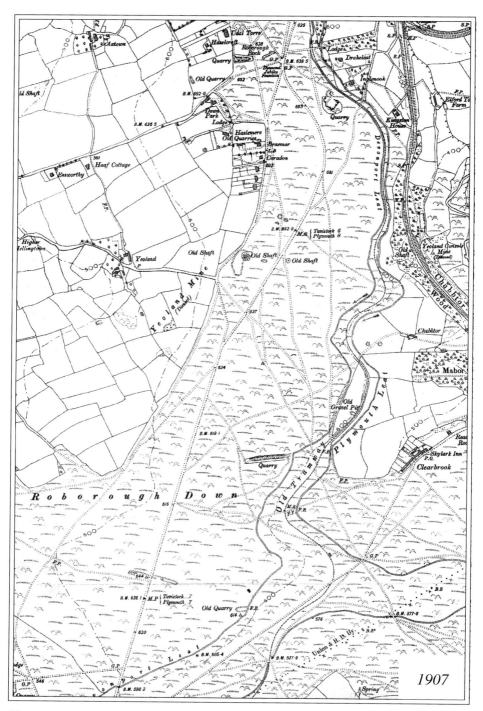

1907

*Around & About Roborough Down*

*Only about 15 commoners assembled at the Rock, Yelverton, yesterday afternoon, for the start of the drift. They had a hard task, and it was not surprising that a number of ponies slipped through their ranks, notwithstanding that the experts and the amateurs had doubled the number of helpers by the time the field at Shaugh was reached. A number of Shaugh men also took part in the drift to claim ponies that had strayed to Roborough from there. Many motorists stopped their cars by the roadside in order to watch the picturesque scene as the dark ponies dashed across the rusty bracken of the Down. Other spectators gathered in the lane by Mr Elford's field, and a few went inside to see the drift close at hand...*

*Apart from strangers, however, the majority of those present were Roborough Commoners and men of Shaugh, who shouted advice and instructions in broad Devon voices as the ponies stampeded to and fro in the field and there was not nearly so much interest shown in the round-up as in the well-known annual drift at Shaugh."* A few days later dealers, who travelled the West Country fairs, were expected to arrive to buy many of these ponies.

Roborough Down again became the scene of intense military activity during the Second World War but only after a slow start. Plymouth was always going to be a target for enemy warplanes so it was deemed necessary to have an airfield close to the city to defend it. However, those in a position of power underestimated the size and scale of the threat to the city at the beginning of the conflict. The choice of Roborough Down as a wartime airfield was not a surprising one as it is an upland plateau, part of which was almost ideal for such a purpose. The presence of half a squadron (four) of Gloucester Gladiators at Roborough Airport proved to be a woefully inadequate response to repel the German attackers who inflicted such immense damage on Plymouth in the spring of 1941.

Debris from the blitzed Plymouth was carted to Roborough Down and used to infill various depressions in the ground in order to lengthen and improve a relatively short airstrip. On 15 August 1941 'RAF Station Harrowbeer', rather than 'Yelverton', officially opened as an airfield in 10 Fighter Group. The name was chosen, quite possibly, to avoid confusion with the already well-established airfield of the similar-sounding Yeovilton in Somerset.

In the course of the ensuing war years a procession of nationalities passed through this airfield which included Czechs, Poles, Canadians, Norwegians, French and Rhodesians. This truly cosmopolitan airfield had, at its peak, some 2,000 men and women stationed here.

It was built at a cost and the alignment of local lanes had to be altered. This old picture postcard view, taken at the '6 Cross Roads', shows the former roads between the Rock and Yelverton. There was also the sacrifice of a number of substantial buildings. The shops of Yelverton, at 'Moorland Villas', were three-storey edifices before the Second World War but, as they lay directly in the line of the airstrip, had 'to be demolished'. This caused so much dismay that a compromise was worked out. The upper two storeys were lopped off, which accounts for their unusual bungalow-like appearance today. Had they remained, Yelverton's centre, around its green, would have been more symmetrical, as the terrace opposite would have been balanced by this one. A large house in Old Crapstone Road, now named Ravenscroft, became the station's HQ.

Many types of warplane saw service here at one time or another during this conflict but Hurricanes and Spitfires were very evident. Prior to D-Day sixteen different types of plane sat on the runways waiting to fulfil their roles.

Inevitably there were incidents with so many comings and goings. One Sunday, during Matins, a Typhoon, EK 211 of 263 Squadron, clipped the top of Yelverton's church. This sent the plane spinning out of control and, seconds later, it crashed in the Meavy valley, killing its pilot.

In another incident, and on a rare visit from a bomber, a Halifax found the relatively short runway too short to stop. Consequently it ploughed its way through the end of the airfield only to find itself straddling the road to Plymouth. There were numerous accidents but nothing collided with the menacing presence of Roborough Rock, sited close to where two runways crisscrossed. The notion that the Rock was cut lower in part to facilitate the comings and goings of the aeroplanes is a myth. Apparently the strange shape of the Rock can be accounted for, as Alice J. Bere wrote in her illuminating 1920s book about the history of Buckland Monachorum and district: *"The Rock on the Down was formerly bigger, the centre portion being nearly as high as the ends, but between 1830 and 1840 a portion of the centre was quarried for road-making."*

The legendary Glenn Miller (1904–1944), the famous 'big band' leader, landed at RAF Harrowbeer to give concerts to troops in the area. He was scheduled to leave this airfield on 28 August 1944 but typical Dartmoor weather meant that take-offs were impossible so he had a sightseeing tour of Plymouth instead and left the next day. Just four months later he was presumed dead when his plane went 'missing' on 16 December whilst en route to Paris.

The airfield hosted an important engagement when the 33rd President of the USA, Harry S. Truman, arrived, in August 1945, in his giant 'Skymaster'. He had intended landing at St Mawgan, in North Cornwall, whilst en route to meet King George VI but misty weather, once more, meant that his plane was redirected to RAF Harrowbeer.

Following the Second World War there was considerable debate as to what to do with this airfield. There were those who wanted to develop it as a new 'Plymouth Airport' and then there were those who were horrified by the notion. The arguments raged over several years whilst, in the meanwhile, the relentless hand of Mother Nature saw to it that scrubland had covered most of the airfield by 1949. The setting up of the Dartmoor National Park in 1951, with Roborough

Down coming just, but only just, within its limits, was enough to help secure its long-term future against further development of this type.

This stone was unveiled in 1981 to commemorate the airfield's past.

Clearbrook, on the lower slopes of Roborough Down about a mile to the south of Yelverton, is a hamlet which perfectly fits the description of being built 'in the middle of nowhere'. It is composed principally of a single line of buildings of which my favourite is the Skylark. It is a fine, extremely popular, public house which we 'discovered' when researching *Six Short Pub Walks on Dartmoor* and also included as a destination in *Family Bike Rides in Devon*.

Clearbrook is aptly named, for a 'clear brook' runs along the bottom of the end of the cottage gardens. Although the hamlet doesn't have an industrial appearance, many of the cottages were built as miners' homes and some, they say, farther down the hill, were for railwaymen. Despite its small size it has produced at least one 'Bond Girl', but which one is classified information…

One of the most shy of all the Dartmoor tors is found close to Clearbrook. It is called Chub Tor, an extra 'b' seeming to be an option in its spelling, if maps and other authors are to be believed. Terry Bound wrote this in *The A-Z of Dartmoor Tors* about it: *"Only noticed at close quarters, the tor may easily be missed. It's near the line of Drake's Leat opposite the name of the house that Hemery gives. The R. Meavy flows on the east of the rocks the other side of the track of the Princetown railway line …The path approaching the tor from the north is shown as beginning near Roborough Rock, but in parts it is not so easy to follow exactly. However if you keep the leat bed close by on your left (east), Chub Tor should be located."* Many people have acquired Terry Bound's book and made an immense effort to visit every single tor, some remote, some magnificent and others, like this one, quite insignificant in the overall scheme of Dartmoor things.

To the west of Roborough Down, beyond the deciduously-fringed edge of the open common, the countryside gradually loses height towards the River Tavy. In between there are some tributary valleys where there are a number of hamlets and the occasional small village.

Buckland Monachorum is such a place, nestled in a depression between the northern extremity of Roborough Down and the River Tavy. Its name is something of a mouthful to say in conversation and the second part has been pronounced in a variety of ways. These two lines of doggerel help to illustrate the point:

"If you want to stagger 'em – Say Monaggerem,
But to preserve decorum – Say MonaCHORum."

Whatever the pronunciation, the latter part of the name still means 'of the monks', which makes sense because nearby Buckland Abbey, prior to the Dissolution, was home to a multitude of monks. In the past the village was often referred to as 'Buckland Drake' after the great Elizabethan seaman who lived nearby.

In 1985 the Drake Manor Inn made the news when it was the cause of some unusual roadworks. The landlord at that time, Colin Nuttall, 'called time' on the old beer cellar at the back of the pub and wished to store his barrels on the opposite side of the road in an old stone barn. In order that the beer could travel to the pumps it was necessary to dig a four-feet-deep trench across the main street. Set within it was a plastic conduit which carried nine pipes to enable the real ales, best bitters, and ciders to get from their new 'cellar' back to their 'spiritual' home.

Just five years later the pub made the news again with one of those interesting little twists of history. Bearing in mind Sir Francis Drake's powerful connections with the village, there was a touch of irony when it came to re-roofing the inn. Its being a listed building meant that the worn slates had to be replaced by natural ones. The only practical and economic solution was the use of Spanish slates! The landlord was quoted as saying that "It does not help that we stock Spanish beer as well". Almost enough to make Drake turn in his watery Caribbean grave!

The church of St Andrew was once described by that famous historian Professor Hoskins as 'the best in the area', and was the scene of an unusual occurrence in 1935. A bell ringing festival took place there and many people gathered outside to savour the sounds of sweet peals being rung. Those who looked heavenwards towards the top of the church could hardly believe their eyes for each time the tenor, the heaviest of the six bells, installed in the tower in 1723, was rung a pinnacle rocked to and fro! This resulted in six weeks of silence as the 'bopping' pinnacle had to be removed and then more securely re-bedded to stop it joining in with the music.

The church has seen some long-serving vicars, a testament to the longevity often enjoyed by folk in this pleasant place. Joseph Rowe's incumbency spanned the years 1646 to 1708, a period of 62 years, Charles Barter chalked up 63 years in the Victorian era and Richard Hayne served an incredible 65 years.

Whilst researching Buckland I found this undated newspaper clipping which was headed "A Village Offered For Sale":

*"The whole of the village of Buckland Monachorum, with the exception of five houses, was offered for sale by Messrs. Glanville and Son, of Horrabridge, at the Manor Hotel, Buckland, on Tuesday. There was a large attendance. The property, all freehold, belonged to Sir Massey Lopes, Bart., and was presented in 21 lots, about a dozen of which were sold. Among the lots not sold was the Manor Hotel, with two pasture fields and orchard, the highest bidding for which was £525, and £600 was the reserve price."*

Not all of Sir Massey's immense estate was aesthetically pleasing. In a *Tour of North Devon*, published in 1887, the writer had strayed as far south as Plymouth and in describing the journey from there to Tavistock had this to say: *" ... suffice it to say that the lively air over the Down was as fresh and as invigorating as ever – that Sir Massey Lopes's entrance lodges looked as ugly as ever – that the church towers which stood on the moorland side stood out distinct and picturesque in the bright clear atmosphere, denoting by their glad existence that the inhabitants of their respective localities were as good as ever, and finally that the lovely Bickleigh*

*Vale looked as attractive and cheery as it did when Nat Howard wrote his very pretty poem to commend its charms."*

Buckland Monachorum has had its share of famous visitors, some helping out with such things as the summer fête. *Are You being Served?* star Nicholas Smith took time out from appearing in *A Midsummer Night's Dream* in Plymouth to open one of them. David Soul, at the height of his *Starsky and Hutch* fame, visited the village when making the film *The Stick Up* or *Mud*. The film was panned by the critics, just one quote being: "The worst of this or possibly any year". It wasn't given a general release but locals involved in the filming were treated to a special showing in Plymouth. More about this film can be found in another of my books, called *Made in Devon,* which is dedicated to the subject of films and television programmes shot in the county.

Buckland Abbey is a National Trust property which draws visitors from all over the world, but it has had a long history as a home to monks, and later to the rich and famous.

When Cistercian monks constructed the first buildings here more than seven centuries ago this was a wilderness. Their order had been founded 175 years earlier in Burgundy, the Cistercians having been a breakaway movement from the Benedictines. Their monks chose to forego the wealth and luxury of their peers. The first monks, a dozen of them, came to Devon in 1278 from Quarr, on the Isle of Wight, to live in much more modest surroundings than are seen today. However, they had access to some 20,000 acres of land which they used to good purpose for more than two centuries before things began to change. Henry VIII made sure that the 'contemplative life' came to a somewhat inglorious end. Within a year of the monks' departure Buckland was leased to George Pollard, for 21 years, but within three years the King sold the abbey to Sir Richard Grenville.

Sir Richard settled the property on his heir but the house proved to be something of a bad omen, for the first three occupants all shared the fate of drowning at sea.

Sir Richard's grandson, a truly great man, so the history books tell us, swept away the cloisters and other domestic buildings. But it was not just a case of doing away with the old, because he added a new wing to the house and developed his estate. He embellished the Great Hall which formed the heart of the house. Sir Francis Drake, a rich man, bought the property in 1581 when he was just 36 years old and at the peak of his fame. It is in the Great Hall that Drake's famous Drum, the one that he took on his global travels, is found. Many years ago, on Channel 4's television series *Treasure Hunt*, this was the final clue to which Anneka Rice had to be guided. What excitement!

Drake was away from his beloved Buckland for long periods of time. Nevertheless, far from neglecting his home, he built up its defences, and improved the water supply, something always close to his heart.

Although there were those who thought Drake to be immortal, he wasn't. He died of dysentery off Puerto Bello on 26 January 1596 and was buried at sea in the West Indies. Apparently Drake is still a busy man in death, and more than 400 years after his passing he is thought to haunt a number of locations in Devon!

Sir Francis, whose life is so well documented, married twice but did not father any children. After his death the house passed to his brother, Thomas, and then down through his descendants, an interruption occurring when Charles I granted the property to his King's General, the infamous Richard 'Skellum' Grenville. The Drakes retrieved their property after the Civil War. With the death of another Sir Francis Drake, in 1794, there was no direct heir to Buckland but the house remained in the family and was not sold.

Lady Seaton, who inherited it in 1915, made it her work to restore much of the property to its former glory. However, there was a major fire in January 1938, when it was occupied by the

Meyrick family, but fortunately nobody was hurt. Mrs Meyrick and her two sons escaped, her husband having been up in London at the time. Fire brigades from Plymouth, Tavistock and Yelverton rushed to the scene to discover the west wing well ablaze. Although valuable paintings and china were lost, some of the house's historic treasures were salvaged; these included the famous Drake's Drum and the sword which Drake wore as Lord Mayor of Plymouth. Most of the salvaged items were stored at Nutwell Court near Lympstone, in East Devon, until repairs were made to the house.

Following the Second World War the house was sold for the first time since the days of Elizabeth I. Captain Arthur Rodd bought it and gave it to the National Trust. However, the good captain did not live to see Buckland Abbey opened to the public, by Lord Mountbatten, in 1951. Initially it was leased to Plymouth City Council but in 1987 the National Trust took over the reins of administering the Abbey. The rest, they say, is all history. Needless to say, Sir Francis Drake's presence still dominates the scene, but that's what you would expect of a national hero in his own home!

If you pay a visit keep a look out for the ghost of two headless black horses pulling a chariot, for these are perennial spectral beasts which have been seen here by many down the years!

Although it may not be as famous as Frances Hodgson-Burnet's *Secret Garden,* Buckland Monachorum has its own internationally renowned eight-acre green 'oasis' of floral splendour. The Garden House, with its romantic two-acre walled gardens set around the ruins of a sixteenth century vicarage, is an attraction open to the public from March to the end of October. Visitors can relax and wander through the Quarry Garden, Spring Garden, Old Cottage Garden, Rhododendron Walk, and the Wild Flower Meadow. This gem in the landscape has a history. At the dissolution, the 'deposed' Abbot was offered the living of Buckland Monachorum. This was his vicarage and it gazed down onto his new church. In 1820 the vicarage was demolished, but not before one or two of the former abbot's successors had made their mark. One of the vicars marked each of his surviving children by planting a lime tree along the path between here and the church. The field in which they stood is known as 'Ten Trees' despite the fact that now there are just eight. It's believed his wife gave birth to a staggering fourteen children but we must presume that some died at an early age, as was often the case in the past.

In 1946 Mr and Mrs Fortescue started the walled garden, and as the years rolled by it was regarded as essential to continue their good work so a private charitable trust was set up. The Garden House has since extended into the six-acre 'Ten Trees' field and is worth a visit, a time for peaceful pleasure, in what is one of Devon's best-kept secrets!

Beautiful Milton Combe, as the second part of its name suggests, lies in a valley just to the south of Buckland Abbey but is within the parish of Buckland Monachorum. Here are some extracts from a local newspaper about the opening, in 1878, of the village's new church, the Church of the Holy Spirit. The religious 'bits', of which there were many column inches, have been left out. Sorry, Vicar!

"Hardly in all Devonshire is there a more picturesque little spot than the hamlet of Milton ... It is embowered in the rich foliage which covers the sides of the deep gorge in which it is situated. Many old cottages with cob walls and thatched roofs occupy the very lowest level of the valley, bringing out by contrast its natural beauties more vividly; and now another and more pleasing element has been added to the scene, as viewed from above – the little bell turret and a sharp-pointed roof surmounted by the holy symbol. These of course belong to a new church which during the last twelve months has risen to completion. Milton is two miles from the parish church at Buckland, and when it is stated that there are some three hundred people in the immediate vicinity nothing more need be said to demonstrate the want of some place of worship within easy reach of all ... The Rev R. J. Hayne, the present vicar, has always recognised this want ... unfortunately a serious attack of quinsy prevented his being present at the services and dedication of the church yesterday ...

The service yesterday commenced at a quarter to twelve. The weather was not all that could be desired, very heavy showers falling at intervals; but the church, which was built to accommodate 120, was nevertheless crowded.

A celebration of Holy Communion followed ... A luncheon afterwards took place in the great barn of Buckland Abbey, which had been tastefully fitted up for the occasion by the family of the occupier, Mr Pratt."

The Who'd Have Thought It, now the only village pub, has its ghosts! One is the spectral form of one of its former landlords, the appropriately named Abe Beer. The other phantom is a ghostly

cavalier, one of many found in Devon, whose party trick is to ring for service.

Having dealt with the countryside on the western side of Roborough Down it's now time to return to the eastern side, and what better of way of doing it than including this vivid account of a Victorian day out in the beautiful, wooded Bickleigh Vale. It was written by Rachel Evans, a Victorian writer with style and character, and is taken from her book *Home Scenes, or Tavistock and its Vicinity*, published in 1846.

"The summer of 1841 was even more wet and gloomy than its predecessor, 1840. Our Devonshire sky was continuously overcast with clouds from the Atlantic; our towns were constantly enveloped in fog and vapor; their streets were thoroughly disagreeable from mud; and the whole aspect of the country was watery and unpromising. People almost doubted the time of year, and were inclined to write November instead of July. However as autumn advanced, the state of things improved; a gleam of sunshine now and then stole through the vapor of the morning, and the afternoons were about as bright and beautiful as any respectable person could desire. So we contrived to take our usual walks and excursions, nothing daunted by the threatening approach of the early part of the day. A proposition to visit Bickleigh vale was not to be resisted; all were prepared with warm clothing to resist the Dartmoor mist which looks more like drizzling rain; and we started in various conveyances to proceed in the quest of the picturesque.

Bickleigh is, at least, nine miles from Tavistock; but we proposed first to visit Shaugh Bridge: so two of our charioteers determined to cut across country, and to find a shorter way over

Roborough Down. The rest went round by the usual road, which turns off beyond Jump. Notwithstanding the unevenness of the road, I enjoyed the drive over the turf exceedingly.

An open carriage gave us full liberty to admire the prospects, and my companion kindly indulged my love of seeing everything, by driving here, there, and everywhere, without much regard to the difficulties of the way. Sometimes a level bit of ground enabled us to get on smoothly, but generally there were sufficient obstacles to be overcome; we drove twice through the Plymouth [Drake's] leat; and the very best road was a narrow cart track full of deep ruts ...

We proceeded in a direction across the [Roborough] Down, and descended a steep hill towards the bridge. Here some of the party were in an anxious expectation of our arrival. A waggonload of gay [cheerful] people from Plymouth assisted in giving animation to the scene. The confluence of the two rivers, the Mew and the Cad [Plym], takes place just by Shaugh Bridge; they proceed thence under the name of the Plym. The promontory of land rising between these winding streams is to be gained only by stepping stones, which are crossed with the greatest ease when the water is low.

I was soon landed on the opposite side, and seated in a quiet nook to attempt a sketch of the bridge; but I found this to be the least interesting object in the surrounding scene. The twisted trunks of the fine old trees, which fling their branches across the water; and the bold form of the granite rocks, which present their rough sides to the brawling rivers, pleased me far more than this tame specimen of human masonry; and I left my sketch unfinished, to wander at will amongst the beauties around. Above arose the broad outline of Dewerstone, from whose summit the clouds had just rolled away. Broken ridges of stones presented tempting

opportunities of climbing the eminence; at the foot of the hill were groups of young saplings, towering above the decrepid [sic] figures of their parent oaks ... Dewerstone rock may be ascended by a winding path on the western side from the base. We chose a shorter mode of gaining the summit, and clambered up by the jutting stones in a strait [sic] direction. By this means we gained more time to enjoy the extensive prospect around. The eye wandered over hill and dale, diversified by corn fields and pasture land, woods and streams, scattered cottages, and clustering villages with church towers rising from the midst, until it rested on the expanse of the ocean rolling its glittering waves into the Plymouth Sound. By the aid of a telescope we could discern the vessels as they rode at anchor in their safe haven. The towns of Plymouth and Devonport also appeared, like small spots in the broad map spread before us. The view is really magnificent, but we were still more pleased with a river scene which awaited us below. Descending the declivity on the eastern side, we came suddenly on some rocks which rise almost perpendicularly from the banks beneath. A general exclamation of surprise and delight broke forth as we gazed on the noble defile, through which the river pours its waters with impetuous violence. The valley on a smaller scale resembles Tavy Cleaves, but the rocks bear a different character, being here, and there clothed with tall grass and brushwood. If we might note the distinction we should say, that the view from the heights above Tavy Cleaves is wilder, but that from the Dewerstone more beautiful. No visitor to Shaugh should neglect this lovely valley, which is about a mile above the bridge, if the path be followed through the woods by the stream.

*The companions ... to this favoured spot were anxious to proceed on towards Bickleigh vale, partly because it was the place of rendezvous, and partly (or mainly) because we were to take dinner there. So we lost no time in re-ascending our vehicles, and preparing once more to traverse the rugged roads; the cart with a bountiful supply of provisions in front, and our hungry selves following close behind. Many a lingering look was cast at the scenes we left, but we paused only once, wheeling round the side of a steep hill to gaze on the old manor house of Ley (formerly belonging to the family of Slanning), which appeared by the river, rising above the trees. The rest of the way was merrily pursued through narrow lanes, above which the woodbine and hazel formed a continued bower, while the wild rose lent its fragrance as we passed.*

*Our generous caterer had prepared a sumptuous feast by the time we had all assembled; it was served on the ground, in primitive fashion, beneath a spreading oak near the entrance to the vale ...*

*After dinner we rambled through the wood to a considerable distance, but found no scene as lovely as that above Shaugh Bridge. The character of the vale is altogether different, being much tamer, but still very interesting.*

*On our return, most of the party chose to walk up the steep hill which leads to Bickleigh village. A handsome inn first attracted our notice, built with good taste in the gothic style of architecture, and affording every accommodation for the numerous parties who visit this romantic vicinity.*

*Curiosity next led us to the village Church, which by its late alterations has made it one of the most graceful little edifices that can be seen ... There was only one thing to regret ... An old monument to the famous Sir Nicholas Slanning on which was made mention of his fatal duel with John Fitz, is gone. Being constructed only of gypsum or plaster of Paris, it broke in the act of removal, and was found too much disfigured to be replaced.*

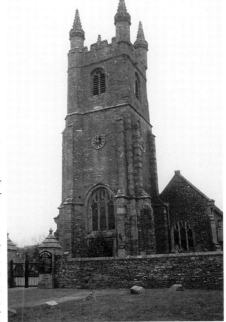

*On leaving the church, we sought our various conveyances, and travelled by a winding and rugged road to Jump, passing in our way Roborough House, at present the residence of Mrs Walker."* Perhaps a little light should be shed on some of the points made in her wonderful travelogue. 'Jump' was an earlier name for Roborough, not an instruction given to any Royal Marine trained at Bickleigh! There were other variations of this local name, these being The Jump, Trenaman's Jump and Tregune's Jump.

The public house at 'Jump' in 1850 is listed as the Lopes Arms and it's still there – unlike the village it's named after.

The inn referred to at Bickleigh, now a 'dry' village, was the Maristow Inn (now Hatshill House), established in 1839, a short time before Rachel's visit, but it closed early in the twentieth century.

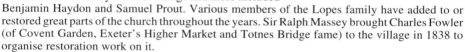

The Slannings acquired the manor after the Dissolution. However, according to Professor Hoskins, in his *Devon*, it was Gamaliel Slanning who was killed in a duel with Sir John Fitz of Fitzford (Tavistock) in 1599. His son, Nicholas Slanning, was killed at the Siege of Bristol on 26 July 1643. Gamaliel's granddaughter, Elizabeth Modyford, who died in 1724 and was a great benefactor, made a provision in her will so that the poor of the parish, not receiving parish help, could be given money each Sunday to buy bread.

Bickleigh's church of St Mary the Virgin was the subject of a painting by William Spreat in 1842 but other well-known artists also stayed in the village and these included Benjamin Haydon and Samuel Prout. Various members of the Lopes family have added to or restored great parts of the church throughout the years. Sir Ralph Massey brought Charles Fowler (of Covent Garden, Exeter's Higher Market and Totnes Bridge fame) to the village in 1838 to organise restoration work on it.

The massive Royal Marine camp of 42 Commando, on the shoulder of the hill above Bickleigh Vale, has been an important fixture for several decades. A pulpit was dedicated in May 1957 to the memory of six of its men who were killed in the Suez campaign. With many relatives present, it was a moving occasion as the poignant Last Post and Reveille were sounded by a bugler.

Beautiful Bickleigh Vale lies to the south-south-east of Roborough Down. *Hints to Tourists – Tavistock and Neighbourhood* in the early twentieth century had this to say of this woodland wonderland: *"... he may certainly with advantage journey to Bickleigh. This gives him an opportunity to seek out the beauties of Bickleigh Vale, which has certainly been a favourite haunt of lovers of the picturesque country for a century past. Admission may be had on Mondays, Wednesdays and Saturdays free of charge. No fires may be permitted in the wood, the reason for which is obvious. All well-mannered persons would observe such regulations ... Here and there*

*are cottages where provisions can be had..."*

And so it goes on, with Bickleigh Vale continuing to be a mecca for those in search of fresh air and exercise. Since Rachel Evans wrote of it, in 1846, the railways have been built along it, at great cost and with even more effort, and have gone again, but the common denominator of human appreciation of the valley continues, largely through walks and cycle rides. The story of the Plym Valley's railway, the route to Tavistock South and beyond to Launceston, is told briefly in another of my books, *Railways on and around Dartmoor*. The station house at Bickleigh was used by the Lopes family as a waiting room and there were stables there for their horses.

Shaugh Prior is as far east as this book goes, for fear of reaching the 'lunar landscape' of china clay country just beyond it. The village pub is the White Thorn, the second in the village to have

the name; the other is now a cottage just yards away but, like the famous Warren House, near Postbridge, it had a reputation for keeping a perpetual peat fire going throughout the year. William Crossing saw it in 1873 and commented then that it had remained constantly lit for the last 40 years. Even when workmen were employed to fit a new grate the smouldering peat was kept going and installed the minute the men had finished their task. *"Shaugh Prior is a typical border settlement, with its sturdy-looking granite church, its unpretentious inn, its ancient cross and tiny manor pound,"* is how Crossing described it.

In 1891 the village attracted a great number of visitors and this is reinforced by this anonymously-penned article from late September that year: *"This little moorland village, with its fine old church and weather-beaten tower, is one of the most prominent landmarks on the Launceston branch of the Great Western Railway, and is much resorted to by tourists in the summer months. Many Plymothians are wont to spend a quiet holiday there during July and August, and at the present time, in spite of the very wet weather prevailing, there is a fair number of visitors in the village."* But times have changed and the common ownership of the motor car has changed all this. Shaugh Bridge still attracts much attention but the village is no longer a major tourist centre.

The fifteenth century church, St Edward, King and Martyr, possesses a remarkable and ancient fifteenth century font cover, which is mentioned in most guide books that include a paragraph or two on the village. It is made of oak, fashioned like a tower rising some eight feet high, and bears some fine carving with oak-apples, fir-cones and vines. However, it went missing in 1868, when the church was restored by Ewan Christian, and became largely forgotten. When a new vicar, the Rev James Baxter Strother, formerly of St Mary Steps, Exeter, was appointed, he was told by his Rural Dean of its existence. Being an enthusiast of quality church furniture, he was determined to track it down. This is taken from an article written at the time. It was rediscovered *"... in an old linhay amidst cattle and chaff, the greater part of the cover in question was found, broken and rotten, and apparently quite beyond repair."* Not so! The vicar had taken master craftsman Harry Hems, a legend to this day in Devonshire church furniture history, along with him and, on finding it, both men were determined to put it to rights. Its survival was a close run thing for the farmer's wife suggested several times that the "Rotten old thing should be burnt." However, the crowning finial was still missing but more enquiries led the intrepid vicar to a house where it was found in 1871 ".. adorning a rural chimney-stack."

The cover was taken back to Harry Hems' workshop in Longbrook Street, Exeter (now a restaurant called 'Harry's' named in honour of the great man), and the painstaking task of restoring it was begun. Renovated, it was brought back to Shaugh Prior with this commendation: *"This interesting work of art is now the pride and glory of the whole county, since no other example of such a cover is to be found in Devonshire, although several of a similar character are to be met with in the eastern counties, but they are most uncommon in England."* The article put forward the theory that this highly elaborate font cover, when originally created, was the work "of some recluse from Kent, Norfolk or Essex."

The church was badly damaged when a terrifying thunderstorm wrought havoc in the district in the winter of 1823 but, being a weekday, nobody was in the church.

In 1896 when the members of the 'Three Towns Blue Ribbon Society' visited, on their annual outing, both the Dewerstone and the churchyard of Shaugh Prior, they made a discovery which filtered through to the press report of their special day: *"... whilst passing round the churchyard ... two headstones, about half a dozen yards apart, were found to bear exactly the same inscription ... and both dated 1780."* This was the cheerful eight-line poem, Georgian spelling and all, which was keenly spotted, twice, by the folks from the Plymouth area.

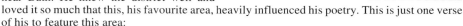

"My heart did ake, my heart did pant,
My blood rund cold and breath did want;
Was sick of heart, what could I do,
And now false world farewell adiew.
Now I am dead and in my grave,
This is the bed that I did crave;
Here I must lie as you must all,
Until my Saviour Christ doth call."

The church also contains a tablet to Nicholas Carrington, the well-known Dartmoor poet, who died in 1830 and is buried near Bath. He knew the district well and loved it so much that this, his favourite area, heavily influenced his poetry. This is just one verse of his to feature this area:

"Oft as noon unnoticed faded into eve,
My feet have lingered near thy bridge, romantic Shaugh,
While as the sister waters rushed beneath tumultuous,
Haply glanced the setting beam upon the crest of Dewerstone."

The Dewerstone is a massive outcrop of rock, a favourite for climbers in Devon as there are climbs of various grades. The Devil's Rock, Raven Buttress and Needle Buttress are there to be conquered by those who have the nerve and skill. The craggy eminence is indeed a romantic location and has inspired many people to write about it. Carrington was particularly taken with it and came here a great many times, no doubt finding it a place of sweet poetic inspiration. The

month and year of his death are etched on a rock here.

Despite the obvious tranquillity of this rocky aerie, it has had its moments. It is often mentioned in terms of the Devil, or Dewer as he is sometimes called. This demon hunter rides the moors at night looking for the souls of unbaptised babies, driving them off the top of this rocky hill – or so legend has it.

Legends of course we can ignore but real life dramas have also taken place here. This is an extract from a newspaper report of a serious fire at Easter 1906: *"On Bank Holidays this spot is particularly popular, and on Easter Monday no less than 1,700 visitors arrived at Bickleigh Station, and the great majority climbed the hill to obtain the commanding view of the surrounding country and of Plymouth, which is obtained from the summit. Unfortunately, there seem to be some persons quite unable to find enjoyment without doing mischief or committing damage, and on Monday the enjoyment of hundreds was cut short during the afternoon by the firing of a thick copse and undergrowth which covered the sides of the cliff. With the fine weather of the last few weeks the dead leaves, furze and tangled weeds had* become exceedingly dry and when lit the fire spread with great rapidity. Dense volumes of smoke rose in the fresh spring air and the holidaymakers on top of the hill were seriously inconvenienced. The fire and smoke were seen for a long distance around, and from the railway station it was noticed that the visitors quitted the hill early in the afternoon, so that by about half-past-five the place was practically deserted, which was very unusual on such occasions ... Having consumed all the inflammable material at hand, the fire died out during the night and yesterday morning presented quite an altered appearance. All the fresh greenness of spring's growth was turned into charred and blackened patches, whilst here and there the trunks of the trees were badly scorched, and in comparison with the healthy aspect of the woods on the surrounding hills the Dewerstone wore a forlorn aspect." A witness saw a number of children experimenting with matches near the base of the Dewerstone at midday and the local populace, although realising that nature would soon heal the scars, were angry about what had happened. Arthur M. Hill, of Ormonde House, Paignton, who owned the land in and around the Dewerstone, wrote to the press to tell people that this was not public property and that: "I might feel called upon in self-defence to prohibit access to the rock and fence in my property, a course I should be very loth to adopt."

Fortunately, now National Trust land, there is still access to the top of these crags and most good walking books include the standard circular route from Cadover Bridge down 'the pipe track' to Shaugh Bridge, the zig-zag climb back up to the top of the Dewerstone and the return to Cadover. It's in *Ten Family Walks on Dartmoor*, should you want the complete route and appropriate information.

The beautiful and much revered beauty spot of Shaugh Bridge is where the Plym and Meavy unite their flows. As we have already seen, it was a popular spot for Plymothians, who would alight from trains at Shaugh Bridge Platform to stroll the half mile downhill to the bridge. Now they can make a similar journey 'under their own steam', as there is a superb cycle way along much of the former line. Although this is an undoubted beauty spot it has witnessed its share of industry. Until the 1960s there was a clay-drying plant here. The waters also generated power for a paper mill, and a ferro-ceramic mine also existed close by at one time. Shaugh Iron Mine was located on the east bank of the river just below Shaugh Bridge and 4,670 tons of iron ore were extracted from here between 1870 and 1874.

Meavy, as its name suggests, is close to the river of the same name, a little less than three miles above Shaugh Bridge. Here is a brief extract from an edition of the *News Chronicle* published in the chauvinistic year of 1939. *"Whenever a man of Meavy stands with his back to the great fireplace in the 'Royal Oak' inn, and raises his pint of ale, he is as much on his own hearth as he would be in his home. For the 400-year-old inn is owned by the villagers, and maintained by them at the cost of a 2d rate. Not many country places have the independence of this little village ... It owns and maintains the Post Office, built its own school, and stopped cars from ruining the village green by a pleasant granite kerb.*

*The oak tree from which the inn takes its name has been stated to be over 1300 years old. It is twisted and split in the trunk and shored up by great baulks of timber, but every year its branches break into green, shading the lych gate into the church. This was the gate through which passed John Loder and Margaret Lockwood to their 'marriage' in the film* Owd Bob."

That film was made the year before, in 1938. The plot was described in *Halliwell's Film Guide* as "A Cumberland farmer's faithful dog is accused of killing sheep. Sentimental yarn with good location backgrounds." But what it doesn't say is that Devon played the part of Cumberland! Another article, this time in the *Western Morning News*, reported on the making of the film and, true to form, the weather had its say. Under the headline and sub headings: "MIST HOLDS UP 'SHOTS' – 50 PEOPLE WAIT FOR NINE HOURS – Sheepdog Scenes For 'Owd Bob'," the article gave a detailed breakdown of the filming which didn't go to plan. The paper's 'film critic' wrote this: *"When I arrived at Meavy there were six huge vans lining the road. Three huge arc lamps looked blindly at the old oak from the green, and a large camera cloaked in waterproofs stood outside the Post Office door. Knots of people were scattered all over the place...*

*Sitting in the corner of her car was Miss Margaret Lockwood, very displeased with things...*

*Once the sun broke through and Miss Lockwood, with the woman playing her mother, mounted a trap, and drove down towards the camera past the Royal Oak. As they pulled up outside the*

*church, two shepherds dashed up past the cameras, shouted 'Wait for us!' and rushed into the church ahead of them. But it was only a rehearsal, and the rain came down again."*

Dousland, on the western edge of Yennadon Down, is left out of most general guide books to Devon. However, it was once much more of an inland resort and boasted several hotels. Its station on the Princetown branch greeted hordes of visitors who were keen to enjoy the great landscape of this district. Today Dousland, a linear settlement, is principally a residential centre with many fine homes lining the road, which runs at right angles from the B3212 towards Meavy.

The Burrator Inn was built in 1880, just a few years before the branch, and was known then as the Manor Hotel, having changed its name in 1960. It is believed to be haunted, by a lady in black who has an enormous set of keys.

Although Walkhampton is a little beyond the immediate Roborough Down area, I wanted to give it a brief mention for personal reasons. Opposite the friendly village post office and store is the war memorial and behind that the Black Brook makes its way through the village. For the most part it behaves itself but there have been numerous occasions when it has flooded the centre of the village.

I first got to know Walkhampton when, as a small boy, in the late 1950s, my Uncle Bob used to take me from my native Exeter to fish (although a more correct term might have been 'poach') in the same stream but just below Welltown. The equipment was basic – a walking stick with some ten to twelve feet or so of light line and a smallish barbed hook baited with a worm. It worked a treat and in a short time it was possible to catch enough trout for Sunday supper. He knew the patch, and the brook, because his father had been the vicar of Walkhampton at one time!

The fifteenth/sixteenth century church, with its tall slender tower, stands on raised ground away from the village and is a landmark for miles around. Dartmoor is known as 'The Land of Thunder' and Walkhampton's church hasn't escaped the occasional lightning strike. In 1909 William Hearder, an electrician from Union Street in Plymouth, wrote to the *Western Morning News* about the aftermath of a lightning blast which did considerable damage to the fabric of the church. The last line of his letter cited the folly of the building not having a lightning conductor installed on it: "If it had been done in this instance an outlay of perhaps £5 might have saved the enormous damage which will no doubt cost £300 to replace."

The northeast pinnacle was struck with great force and large stones, weighing a hundredweight or more, were thrown nearly 100 yards across a field to the south of the church. Hearder's assessment was, "I went up through the tower, and examined the inside; the bells and fittings seemed all right, and the main body of the discharge evidently went down the outside, and if it had not been for the two iron shutes the tower must have been felled to the ground." The same bolt of lightning rent a hole in a stone hedge, turning the granite almost to powder, yet cattle nearby and on higher ground remained unscathed.

Another vicar, the Rev E. J. Pizey, who was the incumbent for much of the 1930s, was nicknamed 'The Crooning Vicar' after singing with a group of children to raise money for the

church bells. An Australian by birth, this sometimes controversial cleric, who had fallen out with some of his parishioners, had the youngest team of bell-ringers in the country. In this picture from 21 January 1939 are Elliott Trembath, Rev E. J. Pizey, Frederick Lamphee, Donald Clews, Henry Coleton, Kenneth Chubb, Harry Bailey, John Methven (organist, aged thirteen!) Leslie Bickford (the head ringer, aged ten) and the youngest member, Spencer Hoare who was just nine years old! The ringers' average age was less than eleven years. Less in the limelight was another of Walkhampton's long-serving vicars – the Rev Walker was a dab hand at carving and in his 46 years spent here was responsible for a lot of the more ornate church furniture.

The Lady Modyford School was given to the village in 1719 for the benefit of those boys who could not even afford the Dame school. The Master lived in the lower part of the building and the pupils were 'educated' in the upper rooms, a situation which continued for more than a century. In 1785 the number of foundation scholars who could 'enjoy' four years of tuition was raised from 20 boys to 30 boys and ten girls. The endowment was to be a lasting one, just a mere 5,000 years! However, the school wasn't without scandal because the Head from 1779, William Shillibeer, saw the opportunity to further his talents, and fortunes, as a surveyor. He was probably more interested in this side of his career and the original tramway to Princetown was just one of his works. However, this achievement had to be measured against his dastardly deed of employing a replacement to fulfil his teaching responsibilities. Despite a petition handed to the Chancery to remove him from his post, he remained *in situ* until his death in 1827.

The school's facilities were extended in 1834 but even this wasn't adequate, so a new building was completed in 1863. There were more structural changes following an unfavourable HMI report of 1893 and the changes have been constantly rung down through the years. The present-day school still bears Elizabeth Modyford's name and her family's coat of arms, said to be removed from the original school house, was relocated on the current building.

The northern side of Roborough Down, once referred to as Buckland Down, is bounded by the lower Walkham valley. This is indeed a wonderful woodland paradise and gazing down on it today, from the high shoulder of the northern extremities of Roborough Down, it's hard to imagine what an industrial scene it would have been in Victorian times. Here there were many mines, which included Virtuous Lady Mine, near Double Waters, Sortridge and Bedford, West Down, West Sortridge (known also as Gem Mine), the often flooded Wheal Franco and the small Walkham and Poldice mines. Hundreds of people gained employment in these Walkham valley mines, some above but many below ground, deep in the bowels of the earth.

The Virtuous Lady Mine, named after Elizabeth I, it's said, was one of the most important mines in the area but as it overlooked the Tavy it has been included in *Along the Tavy*, another of my books, rather than here.

Wheal Franco extended from Horrabridge to Bedford Bridge, and beyond, along the southern bank of the river. Between 1826 and 1862 it was at its most productive with more than 10,000 tons of copper ore being raised, this comfortably guaranteeing the employment of about 130 workers. But hard times lay just around the corner and after 1862 there was a general decline in copper production, as with most mines in Devon and Cornwall, and Wheal Franco finally 'bit the dust' in the mid-1870s.

The valley's scenery was once dominated by a huge railway viaduct, to some an eyesore in an area of outstanding natural beauty, to others a graceful work of engineering art. It carried the railway from Plymouth to Tavistock South across the Walkham valley. Grenofen Viaduct towered about 130 feet above the river and was an impressive 367 yards long, carrying the railroad on an original Brunel-designed cantilever bridge. The wooden cantilevers were removed in 1896 to be replaced by iron ones, and this structure remained a landmark until 1965 when it was demolished, its passing lamented by many.

It was beneath this viaduct that the previously mentioned Gem Mine was worked. The mine's count house was where the ore was taken to be weighed, usually in the presence of a bailiff, who had a vested interest. He was entitled to take his dues, which amounted to a shilling for every ton of ore he saw weighed. However, his frequent visits to the building would not have made him a wealthy person, because the mine's output never lived up to expectation. Indeed, for some it was a most unlucky place. Captain Williams and a miner called Newcombe, a carpenter in the mine, whose father also worked there, were drowned when water burst into the mine in January 1883. It was a danger of which Captain Williams had always been aware and, despite having worked out a possible escape route to higher ground, he was caught by the wave and debris which engulfed him. His body was found about eighteen fathoms from the mouth of an adit beside the River Walkham. Other spring-heeled miners were luckier and escaped the same fate.

Nearby is the beautiful Grenofen Bridge; the 'road' passing over it was once the principal route between Tavistock and Buckland Monachorum. It climbs the northern edge of Roborough Down and is just a track these days. It is not necessary to look too far for clues telling us that this hill has a steep gradient, for the wood which clothes the hillside is Sticklepath Wood, derived from the Saxon word *sticel* meaning 'steep'. There are, not surprisingly, many other 'Sticklepaths' in Devon, a county full of steep hills.

In the mid-nineteenth century Rachel Evans had this to say about this part of the Walkham valley: *"The scenery near Grenofen (a seat of the late Rev Jonathan Phillipps Carpenter) is peculiarly interesting. The River Walkham here flows through a deep valley, having on one side thick and shady woods, and on the other, the breezy slopes which ascend towards Roborough down. This landscape presents much of the attraction of Italian scenery: its secluded dell, and rising eminences, broken by a sudden ravine, and clothed with straggling furze and brushwood, might have furnished a fit subject for the pencil of Salvator Rosa.*

*A turn in the road presents the scattered machinery of the Wheal Lopez mine: at a distance, and when half-hidden by the trees, this usually uninteresting object has a somewhat picturesque effect.*

*Near the ravine in the wood was once a poor fisherman's hut, scarcely distinguishable from the mound of turf against which it is built; where he led, in solitude, the life of a hermit.*

*In the valley below the down is the populous hamlet of Horrabridge. Here a woollen manufacture has been carried on, affording employment to the inhabitants of the place. On the hill behind Horrabridge, is Grimstone, the country residence of J. Collier, Esquire, late MP for Plymouth."*

In the research of this book I did not hear, or see, any further mention of Rachel's 'Wheal Lopez' but one of the several alternative names given to Wheal Franco was Wheal Sir Massey. Sir Massey Lopes, with an 's' rather than a 'z', was described as 'a philanthropist, modern politician and scientific farmer'. He was certainly the major landowner in the area so it could well have been yet another name for this mine. He was heavily involved in the debate as to the siting of a new reservoir for Plymouth, and was against the choice of Head Weir, where Burrator Reservoir was eventually built in 1898. To confuse matters there was a 'Wheal Lopes', still marked on maps, about half a mile to the north of Bickleigh so maybe the great lady was mistaken, misplaced or simply misinformed.

In 1969 an old mine captain's cottage on the lower Walkham became home for the television celebrity, Angela Rippon. She featured the Walkham as her contribution to a show called *Winter Reflections*, the idea being that the presenters should make films about their favourite parts of the country.

The Walkham has provided the power for various industries, there having been the adaptable Phoenix Mill at Horrabridge, rebuilt in 1793, with something of an identity crisis throughout its 'career'. It began life as a corn mill, then changed uses at regular intervals to be used for leather dressing, then paper production, before becoming a woollen mill. To prove that things, like water wheels, often go full-cycle this one returned to its original function of corn grinding before closing down. Its leat ran from the Walkham near Huckworthy Bridge, just a short distance south of the former Wheal George.

This picturesque bridge, and many other places in this area, were featured in *The Country Diary of an Edwardian Lady* by Edith Holden (1871–1920). She did a painting of it in the spring of 1902, whilst staying at a hotel in Dousland, and presented it to her great friend Belle Trathen as a wedding gift.

She kept the diary as a private and personal document, a log that she kept up over a period of years. It's believed that she made so many friends in the Yelverton and Dousland area that she came back every year until about 1910. Sadly, just ten years later, in 1920, Edith was drowned in a bizarre accident at Kew in London.

Exeter publishers Webb & Bower, when they were shown the diary, had the courage to publish it and Central Television later turned it into a twelve-part serial, one episode for each month of the year. The television series used locations in the 'Diary'. Pippa Guard starred in the role of Edith Holden.

The book's success must surely have exceeded the publishers' wildest expectations, because there were sales of more than two million in the UK alone, all helping to put it into the *Guinness Book of Records*. It became the most successful English language publication of its time, this being the late 1970s. It was also translated into fourteen languages and was the number one in the *Sunday Times*' list for a staggering 64 weeks.

An important woollen mill also existed a short way along the road from Horrabridge to Sampford Spinney and is marked on this 1907 map extract as a saw mill. In the latter half of the nineteenth century Messrs Hamlyn & Co, who were "fell-mongers and woollen manufacturers", employed a large workforce. Beside the river was a factory washing-shed which used its waters to wash out fleeces after they had been immersed in a lime-pit. The river waters were excellent for the purpose as they were super-soft.

The Walkham is a fine river for fish and thus for fishing. Close to the site of this former mill a small tributary stream adds its waters. Sea trout have favoured this spot and salmon have bred here, whilst brown trout are a common sight.

The river has been used for the occasional bit of fun as well. Some years ago an inter-village challenge, held in tandem with the fete, saw many of the local villages dabble in a raft race. Buckland's crew failed to show; Horrabridge's raft, 'a last minute job', wouldn't stay upright; Yelverton's crew started well but ended up with two passengers on board being pushed from behind by a swimmer. Walkhampton were the only crew to stay the course to triumph. The picture shown here was taken during a barrel race, just one event of many from the carnival week of 1990. Scaling the weir is a slippery stunt!

Close to the bridge is a salmon leap and on the banks, within a stone's throw, or even a salmon's leap, is the pub called the Leaping Salmon, a building formed from two cottages constructed in the 1740s. The pub has had other names: it was the New Inn until 1951, although at the end of the Second World War locals preferred to call it the Starving Pig. This was because a landlord kept these beautiful creatures but, presumably, didn't feed them too well. Clive Gunnell, whose television programmes on the West Country can only be described as inspirational, has been a frequent visitor to the pub over the years.

Beside the bridge is a fine village sign. This was the work of a former villager, Paul Deacon, then a Dartmoor Prison officer, who completed it in 1989 before emigrating 'Down Under'.

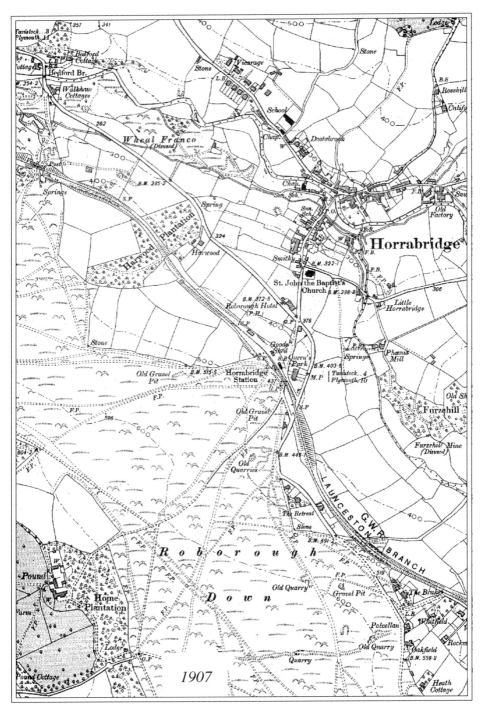

1907

Around & About Roborough Down

The village, the only one truly on the banks of the Walkham, didn't become a parish in its own right until October 1950. A stone in the structure of the bridge, which bears a Latin cross, is a boundary stone and when placed there marked the limits of the parishes of Whitchurch and Buckland Monachorum. In his book, *Devon Survey*, published in 1932, W. H. Thompson briefly described it thus: *"At Horrabridge there is the three-arched Gothick bridge to give interest to an otherwise unattractive village."* This picture shows the Walkham being crossed further upstream during a Beating of the Bounds ceremony, a superb walk of about eight miles, in September 1991.

Until 1822, when the village was effectively bypassed, the main through route lay over the ancient bridge and on into Tavistock.

The opening ceremony of the 1822 road, between Yelverton and Tavistock, must have been quite an occasion. There were eleven carriages and many outriders. The Duke of Bedford's carriage went to the head of the parade but he alighted to mount a horse and lead the procession from the front all the way from Yelverton to Tavistock, where there was much celebrating. However, an eye witness account suggested that the dinner, which was held for about 100 special guests, was not up to the mark. Alice J. Bere, in her 1920s Buckland book, included a letter written to the sender's mother by John Bayly, one of the guests. In it he said much about the meal, which he generally enjoyed, but certain key phrases suggest it could have been much better. *"...there was quite a scramble for places ... the Mayor of Plymouth was obliged to sit at the bottom of a side table ... there was not fish enough for half the Company ... many were obliged to go without any ... there was nothing whatever in the middle of the tables but potatoes and a couple of lobsters ... it was a long time before we could get anything to drink ... there was a bunch of grapes put down but that soon went between five or six who happened to get hold of it ... it was a complete scramble and you were so crowded, you could hardly put your hand to your mouth."* I wonder if he left a tip?

Horrabridge, as we have seen, is surrounded by a large number of former quarries and mine workings. High on the brow of the hill, just a short distance away to the SSE, are the remains of Furzehill Mine, which was worked in the 1860s and '70s for tin and arsenic. It was the scene of a disaster which devastated the local community. In May 1866, seven men and a 15-year-old boy (Fox and his son, Yeo, Elford, Gorman, Pike, Wootton and Thomas) were drowned in the mine. It appears that when drilling on one of the levels the old water-filled workings were breached. The water rushed through the mine and the unlucky workforce, on two different levels, had no chance of escape. The mine closed, after a gradual decline in production, in 1878, with this dark cloud still hanging over it.

The railway from Plymouth to Tavistock South, and beyond to Launceston, gets several mentions in this book, for having come along Bickleigh Vale it had to negotiate the upper slopes of Roborough Down. After Yelverton Station it passed through a deep cutting and 641-yard-long tunnel, more or less under today's roundabout, before emerging just north of Harrowbeer Lane. The next half mile saw the line curve around the contour of the hillside to reach Horrabridge Station, high above the village. The station was a scene of intense activity in the days when copper ore was loaded here to be taken down to Plymouth. It meant that mining companies no longer had to carry their ores to Tavistock for shipment along the tediously slow canal to Morwellham on the Tamar. Within a year of the line's opening more than 200 tons of copper ore passed through the station en route to Plymouth's docks for transhipment.

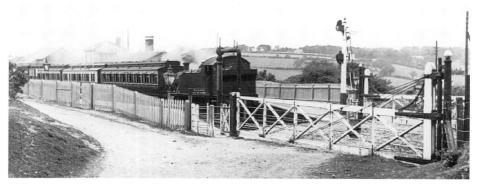

In the few years prior to the opening of the station at Yelverton, the 'junction' for the new passenger line 'down to' Princetown was Horrabridge. The station at Yelverton, when built, did not have a goods yard because the owner of the land, Mr Bayly, stipulated that there shouldn't be one. This continued to give the impetus to Horrabridge which had already become a busy goods station, particularly by night. However, staff had to be vigilant, for the gradient of 1:60 through the station meant that runaway wagons were always a possibility if due care was not maintained.

Various MPs, past and present, have had connections with the village, including Michael Heseltine and Paddy Ashdown (who later moved to Milton Combe for a while), who have both lived here; and the popular, retired Cornish politician Robert Hicks, who grew up here, regularly comes back to visit old friends.

Horrabridge has grown a lot in recent years, many people using it as a dormitory settlement whilst commuting, on a daily basis, to Plymouth and district. It was a different situation during the Second World War on nights when Plymothians feared bombing raids. Horrabridge had been surveyed to see how many people it could shelter in such circumstances. When the regular exodus from the city did happen the numbers accommodated here were far in excess of expectation, the 6,000 or so 'invading' Plymothians more than quadrupling the population of the village. Every conceivable type of space was used: halls, barns, churches, chapels and chicken-sheds.

To finish our concise look at this area we briefly return to its heartland. Perhaps, so far, we have neglected the fact of what Roborough Down is to the majority of people who visit it, an open space to be enjoyed. It has been described by some as "Plymouth's Back Garden" and it cannot be denied that on a fine summer Sunday there is a tide of traffic out of that city, whose inhabitants come to 'play' on and around the Down. Some choose vantage points with views up to the higher moors, then promptly fall asleep; other more active folk fly kites, go for a walk, play a round of golf, or enjoy a horse or cycle ride. Roborough Down's great open spaces are greatly appreciated by the many who either visit or live in this lovely area in the shadow of the upland moors.